EVERY Thing I SAY I Miss The Point

by Floydd Michael Elliott

Every
Thing
I Say I
Miss
The
Point

a poetic memoir
by
Floydd Michael Elliott

Author's Note

Clouds are memories, because memories, like clouds, are never the same twice, yet they are always recognizable as clouds, as memories.

For Richard Greenfield, who gave me the courage to write in the open field.

Prologue

Poet —

O.K. — see

the which way to go —

>*here is paper —*

>*here*

>*is the End of song —*

I Blame Mr. Bourbon & Florida

Teeth

    drawn-in

    by the sight of my reflection

      in split mirrors

fair-weather, or fair-weather balloon, lift

    me away—

          oh Henri —

        We stand harm-

            less

        on crook-

      ed feet — & my son, that son,

        Hiding in the fair-

        way —

Clearly there is a veiled path on this golf course

    a passage

      a way a-

        round?

    [Oh, This Sun, Henri,

          there's too much to it

      & far too much of me]

Mr. Bourbon told me there

        is always

          a way

      around

         Just beware of what

    reptilian things crawl

1

here –

probing & slithering & waiting

    with no clocks to worry about

    except the ticking churn of stomach juices

Henri! Don't let my

    depreciating stillness,

    my quiet reading of you & yours

      Give all of the Me

        away

      in a fury for what I squandered

      for you,

      Henri.

I blame this disintegration on the you

    that I trusted.

Tell them, Mr. Bourbon,

    I enjoyed the poisoning

      of the lump of my

    my hunch-backed prose –

      the fragmenting of my sent-

            enses

    your soothing late night grimace.

Arguing with Mr. Bones

You've come undone

   I say to myself as

I lay out on white linen. The ache

  of the space surrounding

    my head

    pushing in.

Terrible oppressor, oh Henri, you domineer me so,

   you un-wieldy force from generations before &

   I am all silly-putty and broken Lego pieces again.

The depths of my vision still unplumbed &

   I barely scrapping by, my waters too viscous

    to drink,

   to be of any use at all, & those skeptical

rubber-necks looking on as I follow words

     with silence &

then words again &

  is there a law against me yet?

Please, tell my unraveling second-hand-self the truth.

I've got only so many orphaned lines left

   only so many more birthdays to forget

    & I can't keep myself

  from the laying down

  from the pulling of the string

   on my sweater vest

from your gravity.

Crash or Collapse

Walking

through the p-

ark-

ing

lot

I trip-

ped

this body flown past

normalcy &   it cried

out

Inside – be-

tray-

er! –

I thought you

Make me better than I am, Henri.

Make me another *Am*.

Tell Mr. Bourbon to gently take my torn Birkenstock's

off my twisted feet & please

Forgive my left be-

hind nineties habits   or

throw them into high

resolution

& drain my

infection slow enough

for closure.

Or erasure.

Henri, let's lie here

on the white, hot, parking lot

         lines

     bathed in this cerulean sun light–

     this place seems drawn perfectly right here

          maybe too well

     under all these unreasonable circumstances.

             Alright.

     Mr. Bourbon whispers to me that he found out.

     The shell is not immortal &

        our unwieldy cradle has fallen –

        the momentum

        quickens all the heartbeats & all

the clouds wither me through and through again –

     Henri demands I play the game again with my son

     for his mind is still soft and full and innocent

        & if I'm lucky I can capture enjoyment

        that I may distill later

     as an uncompromising sloth

  staring

        from a tree as I chew

        on old memory clouds.

A Christmas Visit

We hide here

    behind the old piano bench

        my hippie totems watching over our

           shoulders, worried —

The brother scanning our room —

    with i-

        Phone camera

        absorbing a moment of what exactly —

    I don't really want to know,

        but it is important for everyone to be

           in the picture.

    The brother in-law, He is the ap-

        parition —

    somehow vague & precise

           at one time

    & I, a hovering nerv-

        ous-

           ness

feet jittering on the red tile floor in

    & out of the piano room

      & do they smell the me,

      in me —

Christmas time freezes & our clocks chime no times[1] —

    & the unloading

---

[1] *"The clock chimes no times,"* is a stage direction from one of Eugene Ionesco's plays

of all the weird presents begins,
     like broken up Lego pieces,
     onto the family table –
the golf clutter, the hand-me-downs from distant cousins,
   the Nerf-gun darts –
   these gifts clinging & clasped & cocooned
   to their old ideas
     of us.
   What brother's iPhone saw is
his repeating mirage
   created through
     echo chambers
    & his dance with this culture's shadows.
His chair scuffed contempt into our brick-red tile floor.

[Oh, Henri,
We're enough – aren't we enough I say –
Feckless Henri
   cover me with
   sweet resin
   sucked from the limbs & the roots of
   this mulching Florida backyard until they leave.]

It never mattered.
And still, all the nice clocks in our house
   are not accurate –
    & Maybe

only Mr. Bourbon finds that charming.

Henri, I'm telling you true, it is here, with-

in the word, that I feel

the most distress —

I am the walk

of the back & forth —

on the freshly painted brick-red tiles.

Only so much of me is left —

my center dis-

integrates before brother's family —

leaves a mess of conversations &

my leeching anxiety cowers

before their indifference.

[Henri, ain't it funny that I don't sneer at myself anymore?

Mr. Bourbon says you can barely stand

to look at yourself at all.]

When brother left

a cool dust settled &

the time felt the same on every clock.

We slept —

stirring the bed sheets a fine mess

Monarch

I can throw a flower

at myself, catch it & the splatter of caterpillar blood –

I can wobble along for some time –

 ticking off the lonely

 as arbitrary & be-

 low the false-

 bottom I lay under. The wood creaks

 as you pass-

 over me

 my Monarch.

 My mouth wants

 to come on out of the grainy finish

wants to tell you in your feckless fluttering

 all you want to know

about the nails, the trim pine –

My avalanche.

[When I hold this page steady worms leak out of the cor-

ners & if they are not worms, Henri, I tell you they writhe

so much like them that my mirror has mistaken them

for the good earth – & all my muscle memory

 strikes useless

cords & the racket of my forget-

 fulness & we are not one,

 we have never been one,

 & I cannot be learned to cry no more]

Cowering in the Metal Cloud

Open up all the clouds for me, Henri. For

    me, alone. I need their interior to be

        my cloak. A shadow dense

enough to situate words

            lest Mr. Bourbon be disturbed.

The noise echoes. The metal core of these clouds

        is nothing but tin & filibuster.

            A need to forget.

    We are all unable. The math

            works out just so

    a balance is impossible &

        because our success is measured

in momentum,

    I stand frozen.

The cloud

    let me stop. If I knew

how to ask I would have asked – but I stopped –

       & the clouds let us drift away.

All of this is a representation of indifference.

There is still no better word for melancholy.

Cloudworks

This is another skunk

hour[2], another late hour not worth

      tracking, except that

                              I am.

     I'd be lying if I said I knew the difference.

I've let myself be-

   come used up. I think we

      do this to ourselves.

                      We   let.

Possibly, there was an under-

   standing once.

[Mr. Bourbon, he's always going along

with the bargain, the bribe]

     But I doubt it. Maybe this really is only an-

       other late hour, with

the skunks gone & despite my pen on this page, no

     real introspection   in their wake.

[I am a Lego building.

I am the bricks in pretty colors

     smashed together.

I am the incomplete house

     when the pieces ran

   out. No roof.

     A door of fake glass.

     A plastic flower.

       A holdout for another's completion]

____

2   A nod to Robert Lowell and Elizabeth Bishop is in order here.

Another Pour from Mr. Bourbon

Start by whispering, &

then never complete a thought. Let the bridges be

    formed in your absence – & burn

    them yourself in spite. Open up all con-

        versations with a question & leave be-

        fore the answer. Never be wrong or

        right, just be in the spot where

            the argument weighed the most.

Don't forgive, and only pay back

in allusions. Give everything & pour another. Forget,

    but know better than to care. Un-

    pack enough for one night only & be

        ready to go, to go

    where – well, you know.

Mr. Bourbon told me, *You can pretend everything.*

You really can. No one has the balls to call you out.

    Or they do & just don't care. You get to pick.

Oh Henri, when first I walked

    with you on a glass beach

        I kissed sand

        I raised pebbles to lips

& shook down parking envelopes filled with change

        There was a freedom there.

Don't worry about the sirens

    in this neighborhood, they are only eerie –

        not scary.   They always drive-on.

Skeletal Umbrella

I have uncovered why the cloud can die now.
There was a soothing lost & the shimmering wasn't right anymore.
When you left, the breeze felt cold again &
the rain ran right through my skeletal umbrella &
the wet-
ness became an excuse
for filled tumblers – for
counting sheep, for another smoke dance with the
green man. There is an understanding
here
between me & the cloud too private to share, an
elliptical note
or a re-
morse. Let us say only
that we should carry our
umbrellas up-
side down in protest –
catch
the rain & throw it back.
& Drink the sting of loss in long, slow, sips.

[I tried to pin you to a memory. This is an injustice – an
attempt to assemble Artifice, Afterimage. All that was asked
for was the warmth of a spring rain from a cloud that only
pretended to be left alone.]

An Almanac for Structural Integrity

When I said —

The cloud can die now

    I meant only of a movement

away from me   You can always have a cloud.

   I see many likeable artifacts

     drifting by.

No, this is really about a re-

   charging. A breeze. A frag-

     ment I didn't want to hold on to any-   more.

When I say "I," I mean

     "we,"[3] so take pause & filter it

through whatever lens is dense enough to dim-

      inish yr perception —

   I want only a feeling

to emerge from the wreck-

  age, the clear image is too

    easy to stumble over & I want no-

      thing but brilliant tracers[4] soaring

        through the clouds to light

         the path.

When we look to the eye to be our only canvas, the paints

   lie drying on dirty palettes thirsty.

[Look, Henri, all I'm trying to say is that

    we all frac-   ture in different

        ways]

3

4

       William Carlos Williams.

       Richard Greenfield.

Counting the Curves in Spider's Webs

Henri —

      My memory is getting so bad

          that sometimes I do not even re-

          member which of these cavernous

            rooms I live in &

   I lay   stalled out

      on another verbal tarmac

with my margins left wildly tabbed & seemingly un-

    done, floating &

      a-

        symmetrical.

   When the fragments are re-

        established as mine

    I can easily claim ignorance —

I believed it was the right thing to do, for

    there is no-

      thing sacred in a labyrinth, except

        time & the Minotaur forced

      to count sand crystals, water drop-

            lets,

the curves in

    spider's webs.

I know it's not your thing, Mr. Bourbon, but please

break this last bit of stale bread for me & stagger away

    the crumbs — by chance I could follow.

Postmodern Soundtrack

It is only a partial truth

that we do not always bury

    our dead. We do not

    need to — they walk

        un-

                informed among us with their

    backs to the wind, their

      hard jaws swollen with

the clenching, with the burden

    of ignorance. You can say no-

      thing to a Zom-

          bie that he hasn't ignored before.

  I will let them dance under the last of the light

      breezes, un-

          der nonchalance passed off

    as earnest indifference —

  If I cut you

      off again, mid-

        thought & between under-

    standing, know it is only

         a parlor trick of self-

           protection.

Henri, I tell you true, I can-

      not give in to this cloud, for its lum-

         inescence would over-

whelm me, leave me shaking & un-
            able to hold us together.
    I'm not even my own

                redemption. When it came time
                    to cower – I folded

                                my hands
                down, glanced

                    at my soul's weather
                            report, thought
            about which cloud

                        to let die first.

                [We all know
                        that I never
                want to come down – I want the drop-
        lets from Mr. Bourbon's night flask to stick
            to the inside
                    of my veins,
            to cascade and careen and rend
                    out the hollow sides
            to give a shape to indifference
                    that's less than useful &
        more than anyone wanted to hear.
                            Push me]

A Weather Appendix

This is the truth of the sys-

tems we allow to de-

fine ourselves, our need to be

with & un-with.

So easy to split

in-half this orange, your atom.

If I asked myself to let the cloud live

that would be bravery enough, wouldn't it Henri?

but you know I won't ask.

Mr. Bourbon has insulated me enough to weather

the storm clouds left-over

after our break-   fast.

Turns out the only thing we have in common is

the sustenance for what we wanted to believe in,

left behind in tattered wicker baskets,

& scribbled notes written in

the margins of my weather appendix.

That, & the questions, of the split-

ting of the clouds, of the half eaten orange,

our atom.

Another combination which renders me mute.

[Henri, why must you interrupt so —

you place me on a beam of light and iron

trick me to balance

& only pay back in expired currency or old checks —

I have issues with you, you need to listen]

18

Between Mr. Bourbon & A Glacier

I just blasted to-
> day in-
>> to sub-
>>> atomic bits —
>>>> It wasn't a bad day —
>>>>> a good one in

fact

but the cork tumbled itself   off   as scheduled —
> & the part-
>> icles of my son's musical debut surly fol-

low —

It is a dream already.

A fogged re-
> mapping —
>> Sometimes, when I push the words just

right,

> Henri lets me con-
>> secrate a moment, or
>>> re-
>>>> frame a se-

> quence &

> place it in-

>> to

His sarcophagus, & enjoy my oldest folly —
> the re-remembering of everything sacred
> Like the son's crumbled Lego's on the red tile floor

— Henri — what use are they now? Have we left our-

         selves stranded? —

    I am the hiding,   the shaming, for-

             shame —

Don't be hiding on my account, Mr. Bourbon snarls —

    You've left the dis-

        course — left it danglin'

           in the mind's eye

     with-out so much as a chime.

Get on down to it, the dirty work festers &

        I know it don't wait on my time.

Henri, The Words can't be called back   down.

    The fresh hardness furloughing

       in my chest — them words know

    to choke the bile down, choke it straight on down

    to mingle in the stomach bar

    to toast Mr. Bourbon & a glacier.

No, Mr. Bourbon, the tile is

     red, the brick is a front —

     you're thinking of

        the pink of salmon —

    the gliding out

   into the air

       in search of extended

breath

       in search of loose defini-

tions

      & a bucket of ice

            stolen from a cooler part of the path.

It won't happen –

            I don't think we're allowed to loiter

                so long any more –

what with Henri's footprints

      all over every note I write & the lack

      of harmonious juxta-position

& Johnny's[5] shrewd Mr. Bones grinning at us with

            his bone-throne all akimbo.

We've broken it. The lock on words was breached.

      When there was no longer a there, There[6] –

         we steered our gaze towards the absence.

I don't know about you, Henri, but I found

      only bread crumbs,

      an axe, spider's webs folded like origami,

      & a vanishing address to a labyrinth

         written on a sheet of piano music.

So much for numbers.

So much for making all this add up.

I turn the faucet on to rinse off this glacier &

      the handle still leaks at its base

      but only when I turn it on –

         possibly the worse time.

<u>Yes, Mr. Bourbon</u>, possibly the absolute worst time.

5 John Berryman
6 Gertrude Stein

Henri, he questions why I must be drunk
        to sustain the self.
No, this isn't a question for you.
I'm asking for those who ain't me —
      why —
It's not a question, only a mere statement of my situation.
Shut up, Henri, you cannot understand
      a situation 'til it be-
            comes
a part of you
        be-
            coming
apart of you
    a collapsing glacier &
      the icing of the self

[I have become the side-track, a drifting cloud that plays
    at believing words have any meaning,
      a place   in
        im-
                ages

    [I am the meaning —
I'm ages of pretend]]

Another Thing, Mr. Bourbon

I don't like always being in the asterisks,

that aside feeling is what you're supposed to take care of.

Do your job.

      This isn't a "please and thank you."

         You need to uphold your end.

It's simple numbers.

A few weeks or years from now,

      it'll be simple numbers still &

         we can't let Henri think it was all me —

            it can't have been

               Me

[You look at me like there is a suicide in motion,

      yet there is no one

        to change the lens to

         a softer focus

Mr. Bourbon says, *Forget it,*

        find some Tiger lilies

   in a corner

      of your heart

      and send a bouquet to Henri

         c.o.d]

Shivers, Slivers, the Son & no Ghost

Oh Henri, how did this hand that holds   fast

    to Mr. Bourbon's soul

become the sticking to the bottom

       of another plastic bag

    of salty slivers

       of crisp or crumpled kettle chips

      in my scrambled memory cloud

All I have is a hazy reconstruction of the restless

        rest

   A moment that ate its time fully & completely

& the leftovers are cloudy biscuit & gravy memories

   worth nothing but the salt and the viscous.

[What am I doing, Mr. Bourbon?

    chase me with another strong glass

      a gangrenous, strong blast

       of compromise

& tell me

   no —

     ask —

      Why am I still a child

      why am I still the child]

[And Henri, vicious Henri, gives me

another ghost-devil shimmering

   in the back of my mind

that passive, brilliant thought jab —

pushing me onto a path of self-superstition

that shivers my bones]

Don't let me want

to throw harpoons at

my ill-fortune &

blame my rage at indifferent clouds

because I only like equations that are unsolvable

because then I still have a chance.

I still have   chance.

Fuck it.

I'll go where you go, Mr. Bourbon.

You've always had the key.

Don't wake Henri.

[Tell my son that he's the nicest person I've ever known]

Every Thing I Say I Miss the Point

I slipped

again into the ravenous

thinking & I crumb-

led

Oh Henri —

I was taught that the moment

when we fell

the ground would carve around us like

rolled bails of straw

& the never ending leaves and pine needles

near my childhood door on Harrison street

would sweep us to an under-

world

or into my own memory labyrinth

of old rooms in bohemian flats with me always in the

basement, cowering

with the mold

hidden in the planks of wood above and the corners below

my corridors always winding

in on my-

self

& the gnawing

Every Thing

I say I

Miss the

Point.[7]

---

7 Ruby C. Williams

Another wicker

basket filled with my debris & bits

of ancient sanity the only nourishment &

Where are you

Henri —

whisper soft, so we

forget the middle

part & most of

the beginning & I

will give you

the end

if

I can,

but Mr. Bourbon says there's a memory pool

so murky you need a

head lamp   to scatter truth

patterns on the

Wall —

to give you a

sense of your time

& of your space &

Every

Thing

I say I

Miss the

Point.

Of your-

      self   across   the flowing of

the anguished   remembrance   waters

     always   else where &

      where are you, Henri?   You

    whose doors of perception I left open

      so that I might cram into my

   small head all the little truths & big lies

& when I for-   get   I

      forget

        hard.

Wait with me, Mr. Bourbon, please

    wait with me in this blighted pool

    that echoes out in malicious ripples again & again

      Every

   Thing

     I say I   *Miss the*

      Point.

My confused desire

   to explain

    a rhetoric

of incompleteness —

My contrition not an afterthought

   but a way to survive your voice, Henri,

   to wallow through a subterranean maze

    of my own making.

[A knowing that I miss the point of every thing I say.]

Bent Nail

These hovels of words, they
     crumble — our wood —
       it splinters
          rots —
Let us burn
    our houses — burn
what we cannot carry —
   'til the nails —
     the nails, bent,
twisted, curved —
   serrated —
   are all that are left.
        I need these spikes —
    they are what anchor
the arm, the leg,
   the why
     & so we save them —
bend them back & make them our
     words, our pieces-of-eight
      our pass-
        card thru
& we burned our houses down,
   & we burned the ash
     that left us our bent nail
      words
we can always find

the wood &

the saw &

the hammer

& make this paper our own

& we press – press

on – sure to see another

vacant plot of land

in this open field of letters –

Forgive me Henri –

I spoke out of turn.

There is only words.

I simply want to

bend meaning

because the truth demands

its own vocabulary

[stare at me all you like Mr. Bourbon–

the page stays the same]

At one point there was some-

thing

called creativity   inside me –

but I killed it.

[I wanted to blame Henri, but we all knew better,

& Mr. Bourbon says he's as innocent as

second-hand smoke   drifting out a car window.]

Pretend Math

I don't recite –

     I can't re-

          cite

the words, they only

make the feelings in my head alive & breathing

       the words are by

          themselves

                    they float

      & when I try & capture

       them

                    I float, too

Yet there is a tugging –

     a reddish tint

        & I cannot endure – oh Henri –

          this last time

     make a story for me

craft a moment of smallness un-

         noticed

Not a caving, or an apology,

     only an acquiescence -

There I can fall into

     myself all

       day long -

I can forgive myself

all day   long

Mr. Bourbon, yes, he's the one

who tells me to

turn off the computer

stop

this wasting of

electricity

& I'm an old phosphorescent light bulb

in this LED

world,

another cartooning of

depth & emotion.

Henri is right to say I'm all used up.
Still makes him a fucker tho.

These germs, Mr. Bourbon,

they crawl over me so,

like apple juice in a sour stomach,

they itch

& infest

& I'm always a good example of subterfuge

yet can't we bury the pretense?

I'm no good at math

pretend,

at pretend math,

at anything logic —

not when Mr. Bourbon has

a high bumper

along my head-

stone

& the math hates and yet doesn't

have anything

on me, or Henri, or this Judas curled along the side

of my bed.

Tell me pretend math is all we need to pass —

to pass around the world's corners,

invisible.

Henri will want to follow, dear Henri.

Don't let him.

[There's been a screen cheat on this memory card, which
cancels out all the power moves and excuses. We could have
been the last of all of them. Instead we chose long days on
couches and sympathies scribbled in lilac and dew and all
that vanishes while my gaze lingers and fortifies and relaxes
overlong and here we are, at a pause, when all I've ever
wanted was to be left alone and hiding in old video games,
in music.]

Chevelle SS [An Epilogue]

Bye bye Ms. American pie[8]-

      my brother-in-law's iPod plugged in to the stock

           AM radio

           & a growl of 454

    a warning, a charge, leading

        the smoke of burnt rubber in air &

do you believe in a

        god above &

   my brother

      you see only the frame

   for the picture

        you believe I inhabit.

The engine roar is all the fun

    for the night

      gun it, gun it in

        the Chevelle SS

          bye, bye

a Chevy, a Chevelle, *a levee*

(there was no levee)

    Arnold[9] only seems big from the air.

There is a thing called self-

    entrapment — hard choices ignored

      for the sake of immediate safety.

---

8 Lines from the song "Bye, Bye Miss American Pie" by Don McLean are in italics.
9 Arnold, Missouri — a suburb of St. Louis

Your mom, our mom, keeps a journal of her pills —
        the most writing she's done
                in years. A way to count time
                    without clocks,
        Another becoming, her own Henri to inhabit.

We are the racing. The Chevelle.
                Give us the coolant leak &
                    an oil pan gasket drip.
            Pistons firing, smoke.
                Super Stock, SS
                    Gun it.
                    Go.
Clocks set to different times
        litter the walls of her
                immaculate house
                    full of the barren time.
Let's be clear — You know nothing of me
        by choice.
Myself — I stay transposed, transparent. A trans-
                    plant in this Midwest.
The family anomaly.
        A circus un-
                prepared for. Another easy excuse for all
                    they'll find broken later.
Gun it.
                [this will be the day that I die]

35

Giving in works.
        For a short space
you can sit
              still
in the Chevelle
      listen
              to another '70s anthem
in this '70s muscle car
      sip from a stolen flask.
You can see the stars pass thru
         overpass cracks – pretend he is
           your brother. Another familiar
      delusion, another part
        of the **bad news on the doorstep.**
        Of her house.
      Her's with so many un-
      comfortable beds. A fortress of in-
        consistency – of anxiety. Of
          the pulling away.
        A fortress packed, the best
          of hiding places.
   My presence
        diminishes the in-
     tegrity of
         the walls &
the clocks on the walls.

It wasn't always broken. The lack of a signifier here

      an attempt to breath mystery in-

           to a mundane suburban land-

              scape.

Race thru in a Chevelle SS

      top down 454

           390 horses

      4-barrel carb

slicks

                  headers custom Super Stock

Be quick –

      there's a hard-shifting into 2nd gear.

      Miss you.

Do you miss you. We can't allow a question here.

      A silence with only the hum of appliances, &

      our suburban greeting card stuck to the fridge:

         Wish You Were Here –

There is no time, no time.

      Clothes hanging-

            over, drying on the beautiful

      furniture unintentionally leased short-term from

        Craigslist & you

      found out the hardest walk is the one

        with the most monkeys on yr back &

      we maybe told you so & we maybe lied, too,

        about under-

standing your choices. So why am I here.
I knew we were out of luck –
I never yelled loud enough.

Dear Arnold,
            you had me at White Castles, a spurned love affair
            with automatic garage door openings & gas
                        station logic
the oh, so precious aching
            need to drink – **_whiskey & rye_**
            drink it all down. Your water tower stands
                        high as we blow by
                                    in the Chevelle SS
top down, gears jammed down, 454
            rumble, rumble, gun it
                        gun it
            tell me about the time you
                        out-ran the cops &
            how long the gasoline smell stayed in the air.

I had to allow myself the space, a dignity barrier.
            Once broken I
                                    fell
                        Chevelle SS   go, go, go
                                    the only fun for days.
These aren't my people.
            A tape loop, a reminder, for when

I get caught up in the caring, in the paying

       attention to suburban

              minutia — now my minutia.

Where can I hide when normal is plastic &

    the stars from Orion's Belt seem to fall

    on me

         dragging with them the

             inertia of the Arnold void.

Let's get out of here, let's go in your Chevelle SS.

      Rev it, punch the gas

         before long the filters

         will

                all fail me anyway

     & my collapse predetermined will stutter

     & shake & stall-out on this Midwestern highway.

This will be the day that I die

     Believe me when I say I will at least act surprised.

     Let them eat their **Ms. American Pie** —

          another   course crust

   across the landscape

       go in a Chevelle SS

         &

             gun it

Acknowledgments

The title and cover art are adapted from a painting by Ruby C. Williams. These are used with permission from Ruby C. Williams, an artist who ran her own art gallery and vegetable stand along Interstate 60 in Bealsville, Florida. "Arguing with Mr. Bones" first appeared in *Lingerpost*. Moreover, it is the poem, inspired by John Berryman's work, that ultimately triggered most of the rest of this collection; that need to represent the inner dialogue of an alcoholic as he swings from his fragmenting drunken self to the punishing critic of his uncontrolled actions. Because of the compartmentalization that a high functioning alcoholic can live with for years (or decades), it becomes almost second nature to cleave the self into separate identities, here represented as Mr. Bourbon and Henri, leaving whomever the "I" is hidden, almost inaccessible in his own labyrinth of self-delusion, half-truths, and loneliness.